W9-AAT-545

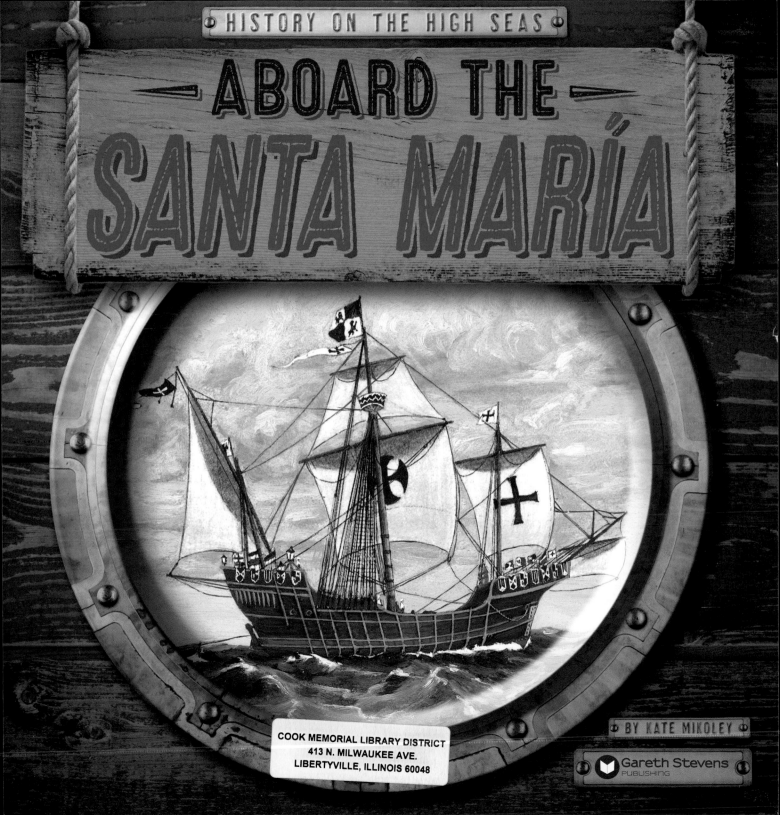

History on the High Seas

ABOARD THE
SANTA MARÍA

BY KATE MIKOLEY

Gareth Stevens
PUBLISHING

Please visit our website, www.garethstevens.com. For a free color catalog of all our high-quality books, call toll free 1-800-542-2595 or fax 1-877-542-2596.

Library of Congress Cataloging-in-Publication Data

Names: Mikoley, Kate, author.
Title: Aboard the Santa Maria / Kate Mikoley.
Description: New York : Gareth Stevens Publishing, 2020. | Series: History on
   the High Seas | Includes index.
Identifiers: LCCN 2019001139| ISBN 9781538237984 (pbk.) | ISBN 9781538238004
   (library bound) | ISBN 9781538237991 (6 pack)
Subjects: LCSH: Santa Maria (Ship)–Juvenile literature. | Columbus,
   Christopher–Juvenile literature.
Classification: LCC E112 .M63 2020 | DDC 970.01/5092–dc23
LC record available at https://lccn.loc.gov/2019001139

First Edition

Published in 2020 by
Gareth Stevens Publishing
111 East 14th Street, Suite 349
New York, NY 10003

Copyright © 2020 Gareth Stevens Publishing

Designer: Katelyn E. Reynolds
Editor: Therese Shea

Photo credits: Cover, p. 1 Bettmann/Getty Images; cover, pp. 1–24 (porthole and wood background) Andrey_Kuzmin/
Shutterstock.com; cover, pp. 1–24 (wood sign) ESB Professional/Shutterstock.com; cover, pp. 1–24 (brass plate)
photocell/Shutterstock.com; pp. 2–24 (old paper) Kostenko Maxim/Shutterstock.com; pp. 4–24 (old notebook) BrAt82/
Shutterstock.com; p. 5 Everett Historical/Shutterstock.com; p. 7 Kean Collection/Getty Images; p. 9 DEA/G. DAGLI ORTI/
De Agostini Editorial/Getty Images; p. 11 (main) T.W. van Urk/Shutterstock.com; p. 11 (map) pingebat/Shutterstock.com;
p. 13 Helen's Photos/Shutterstock.com; p. 15 GraphicaArtis/Getty Images; p. 17 10topvector/Shutterstock.com; p. 19
Universal History Archive/UIG via Getty Images; p. 21 Universal History Archive/Getty Images.

Printed in the United States of America

CPSIA compliance information: Batch #CS19GS: For further information contact Gareth Stevens, New York, New York at 1-800-542-2595.

CONTENTS

WORDS IN THE GLOSSARY APPEAR IN **BOLD** TYPE THE FIRST TIME
THEY ARE USED IN THE TEXT.

ALL ABOARD THE SANTA MARÍA

On August 3, 1492, an **explorer** named Christopher Columbus set sail from Spain. He was hoping to find a new way to get to Asia by water. He brought with him a crew of about 90 men. They traveled on three boats: the *Niña*, the *Pinta*, and the *Santa María*.

The *Santa María* was the largest of the boats. It was also the flagship of the **voyage**. A flagship is the main ship and the one that the leader of the journey usually sails on.

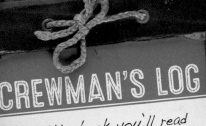

CREWMAN'S LOG

In this book, you'll read about the history of the Santa María from the point of view of a sailor on board. These writings are **fiction**, but they're based on true events that happened on the ship.

COLUMBUS THOUGHT HE COULD REACH ASIA BY SAILING WEST ACROSS THE ATLANTIC OCEAN FROM EUROPE.

5

WHY SET SAIL?

It was possible to travel to Asia from Europe by land. However, in the 1400s, that took a very long time, and the **route** was dangerous. Some had sailed around Africa to reach Asia, but Columbus thought sailing west would be quicker. However, Columbus thought the world was smaller than it really is.

Columbus began looking for help to pay for the voyage in 1484. Finally, in January 1492, Queen Isabella and King Ferdinand of Spain agreed to support the trip.

CREWMAN'S LOG

I've just boarded the Santa María. There are about 40 of us on this ship. We are to set sail soon. It's hard to believe we'll be traveling around the world!

NONE OF THE SHIPS WERE BUILT SPECIALLY FOR COLUMBUS'S VOYAGE.
ALL WERE OLDER SHIPS ORIGINALLY USED FOR TRADING
ALONG THE COAST, NOT ACROSS THE OCEAN.

7

THE JOURNEY BEGINS

The *Santa María* was probably around 100 feet (30 m) long. It had three tall poles to hold up the sails of the ship, called masts. It also had a deck and living areas for the crewmembers. It was fitted with big guns, called cannons, which could shoot at enemies in case of an attack.

On August 3, 1492, the *Santa María*, along with the *Niña* and *Pinta*, left a port called Palos in Spain and began its voyage.

CREWMAN'S LOG

We've set sail! I was surprised we didn't sail west right away. Captain General Columbus said we're to sail south toward the Canary Islands. This way, we can avoid heavy winds.

8

THIS PAINTING SHOWS THE BEGINNING OF THE JOURNEY,
WITH THE BOATS PREPARING TO LEAVE THE PORT.

9

THE FIRST STOP

On August 9, the *Santa María* reached the Canary Islands. All three ships stopped here for some final preparations. New sailors also joined the crew here. It was nearly a month before the ships left the Canary Islands. On September 6, the crews finally set sail again, believing they would reach the eastern coast of Asia.

Columbus claimed it would take 30 days to reach Japan from Spain. Some people believe he knew it would take longer, but no one knows for sure.

CREWMAN'S LOG

New crewmen from the Canary Islands joined us. The people here are said to know a lot about sailing. I might learn something new!

10

TODAY, **REPLICAS** OF THE *SANTA MARÍA* SHOW US
WHAT THE SHIP MAY HAVE LOOKED LIKE.

EUROPE

Canary
Islands

AFRICA

11

SLOW AND STEADY

While the *Santa María* was the largest of the three ships, it was also the slowest. It would sometimes sail behind the other two ships.

The *Santa María*, however, carried much of the supplies for the voyage, including food. It was supposed to carry goods and riches back to Europe, too. One common kind of food on board was likely something called hardtack. This was a tough kind of bread. It didn't have as much **moisture** as regular bread, so it lasted longer without going bad.

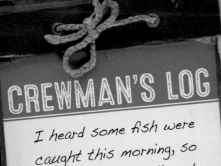

CREWMAN'S LOG

I heard some fish were caught this morning, so maybe I will finally eat fresh food again! That's what I miss most about being on land. I mostly eat beans and salty, dried meat.

HARDTACK, SIMILAR TO A CRACKER, WAS BAKED TWICE
SO THAT IT WOULD STAY GOOD LONGER THAN REGULAR BREAD.

13

SIGNS OF LAND

In September and October 1492, sailors began to see signs that land should be nearby. There were plants in the water. Birds that didn't usually fly far from land were spotted, too. Yet no one had actually seen land.

Some members of the crew began to worry. If they didn't reach land soon, it might be hard for the ships to return home. The winds could cause trouble, and the crew might run out of supplies.

CREWMAN'S LOG

Today I saw plants floating in the water. Some others have seen birds. But no one has seen the coast. A few are getting angry! I worry about what will happen if we don't find land soon.

AFTER SUCH A LONG TIME WITHOUT SEEING LAND, SOME OF THE MEN ON BOARD WANTED TO TURN BACK. COLUMBUS, HOWEVER, WOULDN'T ALLOW THIS.

15

LAND AT LAST!

On October 12, 1492, one of the sailors on the *Pinta* spotted land. Columbus, who was on the *Niña* at the time, later claimed he was the one who first spotted it. The land was an island, possibly in the Bahamas. However, exactly which island isn't known for sure. What is known is that Columbus incorrectly believed he had reached Asia.

The crews explored more islands as Columbus searched for Japan. They looked for gold and other goods they could bring back to Spain.

CREWMAN'S LOG

I expected we would see a city when we landed. Yet I've seen no signs of any. There are, however, people who already live here.

16

MAP OF COLUMBUS'S FIRST VOYAGE

EUROPE

NORTH AMERICA

Atlantic Ocean

Palos, Spain

Cuba

Bahamas

AFRICA

Haiti

Dominican Republic

THOUGH COLUMBUS THOUGHT HE HAD LANDED IN CHINA AND JAPAN, THE SHIPS HAD REALLY REACHED THE COUNTRIES NOW KNOWN AS CUBA, HAITI, AND THE DOMINICAN REPUBLIC.

LOSING THE SHIP

The *Santa María* may have been the largest of Columbus's three ships, but its size didn't help it in the long run. While the *Niña* and *Pinta* both made it back to Europe, the *Santa María* wasn't so lucky.

Sometime on December 25, 1492, the ship hit a **reef** off the coast of Haiti. Knowing it would soon sink, the crew **abandoned** it and made their way to the nearby shore. The crew used what they could gather from the *Santa María* to set up camp.

CREWMAN'S LOG

We didn't have much time once water started pouring into the ship. We pulled some wood from the sides of the boat and brought it to the shore to use for a **fort**.

THIS DRAWING SHOWS THE WRECK OF THE *SANTA MARÍA*.

19

LEAVING WITH ONE LESS SHIP

A few weeks after the *Santa María* sank, Columbus was ready to return to Spain. This time, he sailed on the *Niña*. Thirty-nine crewmembers were left behind at the new fort. When Columbus returned on a later voyage, the settlement had been destroyed and the men killed.

Columbus made three more trips to the New World, as Europeans called it. He took different ships on these voyages, but none would be as famous as the *Niña*, the *Pinta*, and the lost *Santa María*.

CREWMAN'S LOG

Now that the *Santa María* is gone, I am returning home on the *Niña*. The weather has been terrible and the storms quite dangerous. But it seems this little boat will make it.

20

THOUGH THERE WERE ALREADY PEOPLE LIVING IN THE PLACES HE SAILED TO, COLUMBUS CLAIMED THE LAND FOR SPAIN.

21

GLOSSARY

abandon: to leave empty and uncared for

explorer: a person who searches in order to find new things

fiction: a made-up story

fort: a building or set of buildings made especially strong to house troops or aid travelers

moisture: a small amount of liquid that makes something not completely dry

reef: a chain of rocks or coral, or a ridge of sand, at or near the water's surface

replica: a very close copy of something

route: a course that people travel

voyage: a journey by ship

FOR MORE INFORMATION

Books

Gunderson, Jessica. *Christopher Columbus: New World Explorer or Fortune Hunter?* North Mankato, MN: Capstone Press, 2014.

Kallen, Stuart A. *A Journey with Christopher Columbus.* Minneapolis, MN: Lerner Publications, 2018.

O'Brien, Cynthia. *Explore with Christopher Columbus.* New York, NY: Crabtree Publishing Company, 2014.

Websites

Biography: Christopher Columbus
ducksters.com/biography/explorers/christopher_columbus.php
Learn more about the life and voyages of this explorer here.

Christopher Columbus
dkfindout.com/us/history/explorers/christopher-columbus/
Find out all about Columbus on this page.

Ship Model, *Santa Maria*
americanhistory.si.edu/onthewater/collection/TR_325800.html
View a model of the *Santa María*, and read more about the ship on this site.

INDEX